Witchcraft
in Exeter
1558-1660

The Parishes of Tudor and Stuart Exeter

Witchcraft
in Exeter

1558–1660

Mark Stoyle

The Mint Press

Front cover image: Woodcut from *The Apprehension and Confession of Three Notorious Witches ... at Chelmsforde* (London, 1589), by kind permission of Lambeth Palace Library.

Back cover image: 'Woodcut from *A Reharsall both straung and true of ... four notorious witches apprehended at Winsore* (London, 1579), British Library, C.27a11. Copyright: The British Library Board.

Frontispiece: drawn by Mike Roulliard for Mark Stoyle, *From Deliverance to Destruction* (Exeter, 1996) and appears courtesy of the University of Exeter Press.

ISBN 978 1 903356 70 8

The Mint Press,
Taddyforde House South,
Taddyforde Estate,
New North Road,
Exeter EX4 4AT

Distribution through Stevensbooks:
www.stevensbooks.co.uk   sales@themintpress.co.uk 01392 459760

Text and cover design: Delphine Jones, Topics – The Creative Partnership, Exeter.
www.topicsdesign.co.uk

Printed and bound in Great Britain by Short Run Press Ltd, Exeter.

Contents

To Richard and Rowena Coleman,
to welcome them back to Exeter

Preface

When we think of the witches of the English past today, we tend to imagine them in rural settings: in villages, in hamlets, in fields – or on 'blasted heaths', of the type where 'the weird sisters' famously foregathered in Shakespeare's dark tragedy *Macbeth* (1606). Urban witches are rarely considered, but there can be little doubt that, throughout the Tudor and Stuart periods, fear of witchcraft was as strong in English towns and cities as it was in the surrounding countryside. I have been fascinated by historic witch-belief in my home-city of Exeter for over 25 years, and in this little book, I tell the stories of some of the local people who were accused of being witches – and of some of those who were convinced that they had suffered at their hands – during the sixteenth and seventeenth centuries. A great deal more could be said about some of the individual cases which are touched upon here, but this book is intended to be not so much an exhaustive history of witchcraft in Exeter during the 1500s and 1600s as an accessible introduction to it. For this reason, I have been relatively brisk in my discussion – and relatively restrained in the footnotes which accompany the text. Spelling and punctuation has been modernised in all quotations from original documents, and words which have been translated from Latin are shown in italics.

I am most grateful to the editors of *Devon and Cornwall Notes and Queries* and *History* for permission to reproduce material which has previously appeared in those two journals. I am also indebted to all of the colleagues, former students and other friends who have provided me with assistance, encouragement and advice during the course of my research, most notably John Allan, George Bernard, Caroline Bovey, Lewis Brennen, David Brown, Sophie Burgess, Jannine Crocker, Julie Gammon, Malcolm Gaskill, Olivia Gissel, Maria Hayward, Ronald Hutton, and Helen Spurling. I owe a particular debt of gratitude to the former and current staff of the Devon Heritage Centre, and especially to John Draisey, for their cheerfully-proffered help over many years. My dear wife, Lynn, has shared – and helped to foster – my interest in Exeter's seventeenth-century 'witches' since we first pored over some of the court-cases relating to them together in an attic-room in Friernhay Street in 1988. Finally, I would like to thank my old friend Todd Gray for inviting me to write this book.

MARK STOYLE, University of Southampton, April 2017.

CHAPTER I

Before 1558

Witchcraft in Exeter has a long history. As far back as 1302,
a married couple and another woman – a certain 'Joan La
Cornwalyse', or 'Joan the Cornishwoman' – were denounced to the
city authorities as 'witches and enchanters', and evidence of the
deep-rooted conviction that, perhaps as a result of the devil's help,
certain individuals possessed the ability to commit *maleficium* –
or to do harm through occult means – would continue to surface
in Exeter throughout the next 600 years.[1] The stories of the four
women who were condemned to death at Exeter Castle during
the 1680s, and who are believed to have been the last people in
England to be executed for the alleged crime of witchcraft, are
deservedly well-known.[2] Yet none of these women – or their
supposed victims – were Exonians, and the fact that they were
tried within the circuit of the city walls was an historical accident:
a result of the fact that Exeter Castle had long been the venue for
the twice-yearly meetings of the Devon assize courts (at which
assize judges – sent down from London to oversee the operation
of local justice – tried people from right across the county who
had been accused of serious crimes). The famous trials of the
1680s tell us little about the history of witchcraft within the city of
Exeter itself, in other words. In order to explore that subject more
fully, we need to step further back in time and consider the wealth
of evidence which survives about witch-belief among the city's

inhabitants between 1558 and 1660: the period which forms the central focus of this book.

In 1558 – the year in which the Protestant Elizabeth I succeeded her Catholic half-sister Mary on the English throne – Exeter was one of the largest cities in the kingdom. At this time most of Exeter's 10,000 or so inhabitants still lived in the fourteen wholly intramural parishes – most of them very small – which lay crammed within the circuit of the ancient city walls. Beyond the town gates, however, lay a number of fast-growing suburbs, including St Davids to the North; St Sidwells to the East; Holy Trinity to the South, and St Mary Steps and St Edmunds to the West.[3] Exeter was governed by a group of twenty-four wealthy men, who together made up the body known as 'the Chamber', or 'Council of 24', which met every week at the Guildhall in the High Street. During the reign of Elizabeth's father, Henry VIII, the authority of the town governors had been greatly strengthened. Not only had Henry decreed that, from now on, Exeter would enjoy the status of a county in its own right, but he had also granted the mayor and aldermen – the most senior councillors - the right to sit as magistrates, or justices of the peace (JPs), for the new 'city and county of Exeter', just as neighbouring gentlemen had long done for the ancient county of Devon.[4]

In addition to permitting the senior councillors to act as magistrates and to convene the local courts known as 'quarter sessions' four times a year Henry had also given them the right to set up their own gaol and gallows. These would serve as counterparts to the Devon county gaol, or 'High Gaol' – which stood, confusingly enough, in the precincts of Exeter Castle – and to the Devon county gallows, which stood at Ringswell, near

Heavitree. The town governors hastened to take advantage of their new powers, and within a few years they had established a prison for the county of Exeter in the great medieval South Gate and a gallows for the county of Exeter at Magdalen Hill Head, in present-day Magdalen Road.[5]

Henry VIII had given the town governors all the authority they needed to apprehend, to try and, if necessary, to punish those who were accused of a wide variety of crimes – but, at the time that his grants had been made, there had been no statute law in force against witchcraft. Rather than being presented to secular courts like the county sessions courts, therefore, those who had been accused of witchcraft during Henry's reign had usually been presented to the church courts instead. Church courts were staffed by senior clergymen, and it is this which explains why Hugh Oldham – who served as bishop of Exeter between 1505 and 1519 – was later said to have suffered a fatal encounter with a witch whom he had first met while administering justice.

Writing in the late 1500s, Exeter's Elizabethan Chamberlain, John Hooker, recalled that 'in … [Bishop Oldham's] time there was a woman dwelling in … Kyrton [i.e. Crediton] which [was] accused before him of witchcraft and sorcery, against whom he was very hard and extreme'. Soon after he had pronounced judgement on the supposed witch, however, Oldham had fallen seriously ill – and, when it had become clear that his own physicians could do nothing to help, he had summoned the woman whom he had formerly condemned to his bedside, clearly hoping that her magical art would be able to save him when conventional medicine had not. Alas for Oldham, his hopes had proved misplaced. Once the resentful woman had been ushered into the bishop's sick-room, Hooker records, she told him to repeat the following words after her: "Hugh Oldham by thy full name, Arise up in God's name!" which he did, and therewith he arose up in his bed, then said she, "and lie there down again [in] the devil's name!", and so he did, but what virtue so ever was in her charm, he never recovered nor rose out of his bed after'. Hooker – who was himself a devout Protestant – piously went on to observe that, if this story were true, then the Catholic bishop had received his just deserts, '[for] that, contrary to God's commandment[s] … he would seek to such persons for remedy'.[6]

Hooker's criticism of the unfortunate bishop for his alleged readiness to ignore the biblical condemnation of witchcraft and avail himself of the services of a 'witch' not only illustrates the yawning gulf which existed between English religious attitudes during the pre-Reformation and post-Reformation eras, but also reminds us that the all-out assault which had been launched against the Catholic Church by Henry VIII and his son, Edward VI, during the mid-sixteenth century had almost certainly influenced attitudes towards witchcraft, too. There is no space to explore this complicated subject in detail here, but most historians agree that – partly because of the religious antagonisms which the Reformation had stirred-up – the fear of witchcraft had begun to intensify across England as a whole during the 1540s and 1550s.[7] The fact that, in April 1558, the city magistrates were informed that a certain Thomas Weare was 'a charmer and a witchcraft user' is possibly an indication that Exeter was beginning to be affected by this national trend.[8] Following the accession of Elizabeth I later that year, moreover, references to alleged cases of witchcraft would become more numerous in the local records.

CHAPTER II

The Reign of Elizabeth I

In August 1561, for example, a group of witnesses appeared at the bishop's court to testify about the accusations which a certain Richard Gyfford had recently made against a woman named Melior Berdall, of St Thomas parish: just across the River Exe from the city proper. Several of the witnesses reported that, while drinking in an alehouse near West Gate, Gyfford – who was locked in dispute with Berdall over a piece of land – had claimed that his adversary was a witch. Another witness was more specific still, informing the court that Gyfford had told him that – on a recent journey to the nearby village of Brampford Speke – he had twice been in danger of his life as he passed over a bridge, and had 'affirmed that Melior Berdall ... was the cause thereof, and that she was a witch, and that ... [he] would have some of her blood ... for [that] she had bewitched him'.[9] These final words are particularly intriguing because they show that Gyfford subscribed to the contemporary belief that, if one had been cursed by a witch, then the most effective way of breaking the enchantment was to hunt the witch down, and to draw blood from him or her with a needle or a pin: a practice which was known as 'scratching'.[10]

A few months later, mutterings about alleged 'witches' were again heard in the city, this time during a meeting of the magistrates at the Guildhall. In October 1561, the JPs' attention was drawn to a woman named Frances Dyrym – possibly a resident of the district around North Gate – who, they were reminded, had 'for her unquiet life among her neighbours and for her suspected witchcraft heretofore used ... been ... [frequently] rebuked and punished, as also exiled out of this city'. Yet, despite having been officially turned out of Exeter at least once, the JPs were informed, Dyrym had returned again 'and does remain within this city, living in her former unquiet life'. The description of Dyrym as one who lived an 'unquiet life among her neighbours' strongly suggests that she had a reputation as 'a scold' – that is to say, as a quarrelsome person – as well as a witch, and the JPs promptly ordered that this unruly woman should be banished from Exeter for good.[11]

During the following year, a considerable stir was caused in Exeter by the angry words and violent actions of a merchant named Thomas Marshall, who is known to have been ill at the time and who may well have blamed his health problems on witches. In May 1562 Marshall was brought before the magistrates and accused of abusing 'Old Mistress Tothill' in the street, calling her 'bawd, queen, [i.e. a prostitute] witch and whore'. Probably because Marshall was a habitual trouble-maker, whereas 'Mistress Tothill' was a well-off and – as far as we can tell – entirely respectable woman, the justices were swift to demonstrate that, on this occasion, their sympathies lay, not with the man who had made the accusation of witchcraft, but with the woman whom he had accused. They ordered that – for abusing Tothill, and for insulting a city officer who had tried to intervene – Marshall should be sent to prison for 40 days and 'bound over to be of good behaviour' (in other words, forced to enter into a formal agreement to behave himself in future, on pain of paying a

substantial fine if he broke his word).[12] This was not to be the end
of the affair, however, for just three days later, one of Marshall's
own servants came forward to inform the justices that the verbal
assault which her master had launched against Mistress Tothill
paled into insignificance when compared with the physical assault
which he had launched against another woman whom he claimed
to be a 'witch' a few months before.

According to Anne Borough, Marshall's 22 year-old maid
servant, the merchant had slipped out of his house one evening
'about a quarter of a year past', and – after having made his way to
the suburban part of Holy Trinity parish – had inflicted a savage
beating on a woman named 'Maud' who lived 'upon the hollow
way without the South Gate'. Anxious that he might have dropped
the pommel of his dagger at the scene of the crime, Marshall had
subsequently ordered Anne to go down to Maud's house to see
if she could find it. When she had arrived on the scene, the maid
servant informed the JPs, she had seen Marshall's victim, 'who was
then hurt very much'. And when, two days later, the passing bell
had been rung within the city for someone who was on the point
of dying, and Marshall had been told, wrongly, that it was ringing
for Maud, he had callously replied 'It is no matter; it is but an old
witch gone'.[13]

Anne's testimony presented her master in a most unpleasant
light, and at the time that she came forward, the magistrates'
sympathies seem to have lain entirely with Marshall's female
victim, rather than with the merchant himself. A year later,
however, evidence emerged to show, first, that the antagonism
between Marshall and Maud had continued to fester, and, second,
that the magistrates no longer regarded Maud herself as entirely

blameless. In July 1563 'Matilda Parke, the wife of Roger Parke' was bound over to be of good behaviour 'towards Eleanor, the wife of Thomas Marshall', until the next meeting of the quarter sessions court, while the Marshalls were likewise bound over to be of good behaviour towards Matilda.[14] Matilda Parke was almost certainly the woman whom Marshall had attacked in 1562 – 'Matilda' is the Latin form of the English name 'Maud' – and the fact that the JPs had bound her over to prevent her from quarrelling with the Marshalls suggests that, if the couple were continuing to menace Maud – perhaps by accusing her of witchcraft – then she was somehow contriving to menace them back: perhaps by declaring that she would, indeed, put a curse upon them.

The magistrates would have had good reason to take accusations of witchcraft with particular seriousness in July 1563, for in the session of parliament which had come to an end in London a few months before, MPs had passed a new statute against 'conjurations, enchantments and witchcrafts'. Probably inspired, at least in part, by a desire to protect the young Queen Elizabeth herself from any potential occult attacks, this statute had made witchcraft a secular offence, and had ordered that, from 1 June 1563 onwards, anyone found guilty of killing another person through the use of enchantments should be hanged, and that anyone found guilty of injuring people or goods through the same dark arts should suffer a year's imprisonment for a first offence and death for a second.[15] Magistrates across the kingdom now had a clear duty both to try and to punish suspected witches and – because of this sudden turn in events – Maud Parke would soon find her troubles in Exeter worsening.

In October 1565 it was noted in the city court records that

'Matilda Parke' had been arrested on suspicion of using 'magic art'. The precise details of Maud's offence(s) do not survive, so we cannot be sure whether she had been brought before the court as a result of fresh allegations made against her by the Marshalls, or because someone quite different had accused her of being a witch. What we do know is that Maud was tried and found guilty. Following the passage of the new witchcraft act, the magistrates could well have proceeded to condemn Maud to imprisonment, or even to death, but in the end they chose neither option. A few days later, it was recorded that 'order ... [had been] taken with Maud Parke that she shall depart henceforth out of this city within these three weeks at the furthest and from thenceforth she [is] never to return'. In the case of Maud Parke, then, just as in the case of Frances Dyrym a few years before, the JPs had clearly decided that banishment was the most appropriate way of ridding Exeter of supposed witches. But unfortunately for all concerned, Maud either never left Exeter, or returned within a few weeks of being turned out, for in December 1565, she was dragged before the justices once again. This time, she was said to have bewitched a certain Joanna Clarke of Holy Trinity parish and to have caused her to suffer excruciating pain in all of her limbs.[16]

In April 1566 Maud was formally arraigned at the Guildhall on a charge of witchcraft. Nor was she the only alleged witch to appear in the dock that day, for a second woman – one Alice Meade of Exmouth, widow – was also brought before the court and charged with having murdered an Exeter man through occult art. These two cases must have caused a sensation throughout the city, and we know that both women were found guilty.[17] Under the terms of the new act, Parke – and perhaps Meade, too – now stood in imminent peril of the noose and it may well be that either one or both of them were hanged at the city gallows soon afterwards. It is also possible, however, that the JPs – who had already shown leniency to Parke in 1565 – somehow contrived to save the two convicted women from suffering the full extremity of the law. Whatever the case, this double witch-trial almost certainly raised the profile of witchcraft in Exeter higher than it had ever been before – and the excitement caused by the two cases may conceivably help to explain why, in August 1566, a Dorset man named John Walsh was apprehended and subjected to detailed questioning by the bishop's officials in the sheriff's prison near Exeter on suspicion of being a 'sorcerer'.[18]

The statements which Walsh made under interrogation were subsequently reproduced in a pamphlet published in London, and, as a result, his case is one of the most famous in the history of English witchcraft. Because Walsh claimed that he used his powers to heal, rather than to curse – and because the testimony which he gave related to his attempts to relieve the suffering of bewitched people in general, rather than of bewitched people in Exeter in particular – his story will not be considered in depth here. It is worth noting, however, that during the course of his interrogation, Walsh made it clear, first, that he believed that witches employed 'familiars' – that is to say, evil spirits in the shape of small animals – in order to harm their enemies; second, that he believed that it was especially common for these malefic spirits to assume the form of toads; and third, that he believed that 'black fairies', as well as witches, possessed the ability to hurt people through magical means.[19] As we shall see, these were all beliefs which were to surface again in testimonies made against alleged witches in Exeter during the 1600s.

That Walsh was simply questioned in the bishop's court – rather than being committed to formal trial before the secular magistrates – almost certainly reflected the fact that he was not accused of having attempted to harm anyone through his magical art. Indeed, he went out of his way to present himself as an enemy of malefic witches. Walsh may well have escaped with a trifling punishment, therefore, but, fifteen years later, an Exeter woman who was accused of wielding occult powers for the darkest of purposes was to suffer the ultimate penalty. In April 1581 Thomasine Shorte, the wife of Robert Shorte, was brought before the city court and charged with murdering the wife, son and daughter of a weaver from Exe Island - the area just without the West Gate – through the use of enchantments. Shorte had a distinctly chequered past. A resident of the suburban parish of St Sidwells, which had a reputation for unruliness and disorder, she had caught the attention of the magistrates on several occasions before. In 1561, for example, the JPs had noted, with evident displeasure, that a young woman who had recently been banished from the city for sexual misconduct had returned again, and was now living 'without East Gate at one Thomasine Shortes house'. In 1562, moreover, Thomasine had been one of a group of four Exeter women whom the JPs had ordered to be towed at the stern of a boat through the River Exe at North Exe – near the present-day Mill-on-the-Exe pub – as an extremely public and humiliating punishment for their 'scolding'.[20]

Thomasine Shorte would scarcely have been regarded as a woman of good character, therefore, and, after she had been brought before the court at the Guildhall and charged with bewitching three people to death, she was swiftly found guilty and condemned to be hanged. The sentence was almost certainly executed at the city gallows a few weeks later, and in May the burial took place in St Sidwell's churchyard of a woman whom the parish clerk described simply as 'Tamson Sharte, *suspensus*': i.e. as 'Thomasine Shorte, who was hanged'.[21] She is the first person who is known to have been executed for the supposed crime of witchcraft, not only in Exeter but in the whole of South West England. The harsh sentence which was passed upon Shorte may partly have reflected the judges' perception that her crimes had been especially serious – but her pre-existing reputation as a disorderly woman can have done nothing to help her case.

Twenty years later, the magistrates found themselves sitting in judgement on a second alleged witch from St Sidwell's parish. In 1602 Joanna Brice – the wife of William Brice, of St Sidwells, labourer – was accused, like Shorte before her, of having murdered three local people through occult means, the supposed killings having taken place at various times over the previous six years. Like Shorte, Brice was tried at the Guildhall, and, like her, she appears to have been regarded with great suspicion by the jurors, who pronounced all of the formal charges – or 'indictments' - which had been brought against her to be 'true', or accurate, ones. While Shorte is definitely known to have been hanged for her alleged crimes, however, Brice appears to have escaped the gallows by the skin of her teeth, for, while an endorsement on one of the indictments reads, '*she is guilty … and she is to be hanged*', that endorsement was later altered to read '*not guilty*' instead.[22] Why Joanna Brice was reprieved at the eleventh hour, when Thomasine Shorte had not been, we will probably never know.

CHAPTER III

The Reign of James I

Following the death of Queen Elizabeth in 1603, and her replacement on the English throne by King James VI of Scotland – or by King James I of England, as he was now known to the south of the border – there was a renewed surge of interest in witchcraft among the English ruling elite. James had long been anxious about the supposed threat posed by witches. In Scotland, he had personally participated in witch-trials and in 1597 he had gone so far as to publish an entire book about witches and witchcraft: a book which had been reprinted in London soon after his accession to the English throne.[23] Some of James's English subjects may therefore have believed that, by demonstrating their own opposition to the wicked practices of witches, they would win favour with their new monarch. And this in turn may well help to explain why – during the first parliament of James's reign, in 1604 – MPs passed a new act against witchcraft: one which repealed the Elizabethan act of 1563, and replaced it with provisions designed 'for the better restraining [of] the said offences, and [the] more severe punishing [of] the same'. From now on, anyone found guilty of *maleficium* was to be executed forthwith.[24] It would not be long before an Exeter 'witch' would suffer under the provisions of the new act.

Richard Wilkyns, of Holy Trinity parish, labourer, was a man who had long been vehemently suspected of witchcraft by

his neighbours. In 1600 he had been formally indicted at the
Guildhall on a charge of having bewitched a woman to death, and
although Wilkyns had escaped with his life on that occasion, the
rumours about him had continued to spread. It was later alleged
that, in 1606, Wilkyns had bewitched a second woman, in Trinity
parish, as a result of which she too had died. Over the following
three years, he was said to have used his enchantments to kill ten
pigs in St Sidwells and a horse and a cow in Trinity. Still worse,
he was said to have bewitched a man in Trinity and two women
in St Sidwells, with the result that they had all become seriously
ill. The final straw came in June 1610, when another man died in
St Mary Arches parish, in the very heart of Exeter, after having
allegedly been bewitched by Wilkyns. Soon afterwards, Wilkyns
was committed to the gaol.[25]

At the next sessions, which took place on 9 July, eight separate
charges were presented against Wilkyns. The jurors were clearly
convinced that he was, indeed, a witch, and recorded a guilty
verdict on each charge – except, oddly enough, on the one which
related to the pigs. Confronted with this mass of evidence, the JPs
felt no compunction about passing sentence of death on Wilkyns
straight away. In the court records, the grim annotation 'guilty
... to be hanged' appears firmly above the labourer's name – and,
probably because of the horror which Wilkyns's supposed crimes
had caused, his execution took place just two days later. On 12
July 1610 Wilkyns was dragged from South Gate prison to the
gallows at the Magdalen. Sentence was duly carried out and later
that day the following entry was made in the parish register of
St Sidwells: 'the 12th day of July was buried Richard Wilkyns ...
executed at the Maudlins for witchcraft'.[26] It is a poignant fact that

22

Wilkyns's body should eventually have been laid to rest in the very same churchyard in which his fellow 'witch', Thomasine Shorte, had been buried some 30 years before – and his body, like hers, probably rests there still.

As James I's reign wore on, the king himself – while still convinced of the reality of witchcraft – was becoming increasingly sceptical about many of the reports concerning the alleged activities of witches which reached his ears. This was chiefly because, after having investigated the cases of a number of individuals who claimed to have been bewitched, the king had come to the conclusion that these were cases of imposture and that the supposed victims had simply invented their stories for a variety of selfish reasons. A tragedy which occurred in Leicestershire in 1616 – when nine people were executed as witches on the testimony of a twelve-year old boy who later admitted his evidence to have been false – may well have been particularly important in alerting the king to the ease with which both judges and juries could be misled when it came to cases of supposed witchcraft.[27] Yet, if James was gradually revising some of his earlier opinions – and coming to see the need for scrupulous care when trying those who were accused of occult crimes – in Exeter, as across England as a whole, the popular fear of witches remained as deep-seated as ever.

In 1614 whispers began to circulate in the city about the sinister activities of Elizabeth Crosse, the wife of John Crosse, blacksmith, who was, again, a resident of St Sidwells, and lived just outside East Gate. In July 1614, Elizabeth was said to have bewitched a certain Juliana Slocombe of St Sidwells, 'spinster': possibly a very young woman or a child. As a result, Juliana had become 'perilously ill', and it may well have been her sad condition – and the conviction that Elizabeth was responsible for it – which now caused local fears to attach themselves to Crosse's husband, too. In November that year, or so it was later claimed, John Crosse bewitched a number of pigs belonging to Richard Patye of St Sidwells, baker, causing all of the animals to sicken. Meanwhile, Juliana Slocombe had continued to 'languish' and in December 1614 she died. Juliana's death can only have served to heighten the growing suspicions that Elizabeth Crosse was a witch, and when Patye's wife, Margaret, fell seriously ill in April 1615, she laid the blame for her plight at Crosse's door. Complaints were now made to the justices and in July 1615 both John and Elizabeth Crosse were formally charged with witchcraft at the city court.[28]

At the time that the charges were brought, it was only five years since Richard Wilkyns had been executed. The Crosses were now in grave peril of their lives, therefore, but, fortunately for them, the members of the grand jury – the body which was responsible for determining which cases should and should not proceed to trial – were clearly unconvinced by much of the evidence which had been produced against the blacksmith and his wife. Of the three indictments which had been drawn up against the Crosses, two – those relating to the supposed bewitching of Margaret Patye and of Richard Patye's pigs – are endorsed with the single word 'ignoramus', showing that the grand jurors had decided to throw them out. John Crosse was now off the hook, therefore, but his wife may not have been, for the third indictment – that which relates to Elizabeth's supposed bewitching of Juliana Slocombe – bears no endorsement. This leaves open the possibility that the third indictment was found to be a 'true bill' and that Elizabeth was duly tried for witchcraft. Indeed, the fact that – in a testimony which he was later to give in 1625 – Richard Patye made specific reference to 'the arraignment of Crosse his wife' some years before makes it seem almost certain that this was the case. Yet, if Elizabeth did undergo a formal trial in July 1615, she was clearly found not guilty and released, for in 1619 she resurfaces in the court records in connection with an unrelated case.[29]

Most of the evidence which we have examined in this book so far comes from formal Latin indictments which were drawn up against people who were accused of witchcraft in the city court between 1560 and 1615. Fascinating as these documents are, they adhere to a highly formulaic pattern and therefore tell us much less than we would like about precisely how suspected witches were viewed in Tudor and Stuart Exeter. Fortunately, a number of sworn statements of evidence, made before the JPs, which relate to cases of witchcraft in Exeter after 1618 still survive, and these 'depositions' are full of vivid detail. Among them are several which relate to Mary Stone, an Exeter widow who came to the justices' attention on two separate occasions in 1619 and 1620. In February 1619, firstly, the JPs were informed that Stone had been chased by a man named Thomas Bartlett, who had not only brandished a knife at the frightened woman and accused her of being a witch but had also threatened to have her 'burned before the next assizes'.[30] Bartlett's words suggest that, like many of his contemporaries, he mistakenly believed that the punishment for convicted witches was to be burnt – as English 'witches' had very occasionally been in the past – rather than to be hanged, as had been the case since the passage of the 1563 statute.[31] His words

25

also hint that, by this time, it may have become standard practice for those who were formally charged with witchcraft in Exeter to be tried by the assize judges, at the twice-yearly assizes, rather than by the city JPs acting alone, as had been the case for at least part of Elizabeth's reign.[32]

By chasing Stone with a knife, and by issuing violent threats against her, Bartlett had put himself entirely in the wrong, and it seems probable that, in the immediate aftermath of the incident, Stone was regarded by the justices as the injured party, just as Maud Parke had been when she had first been attacked by Thomas Marshall 60 years before. In the case of Stone, though, just as in the case of Parke, it did not take long for gossip and rumour to transform the victim into a perceived occult aggressor, nor for informal denunciations to lead to formal accusations to the JPs. In August 1620 six women came forward to testify against Mary Stone, accusing her of 'wasting' chickens, of infesting a household with lice, of threatening and hurting a number of individuals, and of killing a man by bewitching him and causing him to fall as he passed through a field-stile.[33]

Several of the witnesses' testimonies indicate that Stone was thought to possess a 'familiar spirit' who carried out malicious acts on her behalf, of the type which John Walsh had described in 1566. This suspicion plainly emerges from the statements made by a certain 'Gertrude', for example, who was the maid of a well-to do Exeter woman named Eleanor Chappel. Gertrude told the JPs that, a few months ago, Stone had come to her mistress's house, as she was evidently accustomed to do – perhaps in the hope of receiving charity – but that 'her … mistress [had] entreated the said Widow Stone not to come any more to her house, because people had told her that she was a bad woman'. Understandably upset by this, Stone had then, according to Gertrude, seized Chappel's arm, and declared 'O Mistress, if you forsake me too, then we shall have some doings.'[34] These words clearly demonstrate the despair which Stone had felt upon hearing that her burgeoning reputation as a witch had caused Chappel – as well as other persons unknown – to disown her, but the reference to the unspecified 'doings' which would follow from Chappel's rejection of her could well have been interpreted as a barely-veiled threat.

Sure enough, the maid went on, that very night her mistress's arm had begun to swell up in the place where Stone had clutched it. More sinister still, Gertrude added, a short time afterwards, 'a rat came into her mistress's court [or backyard], and followed her mistress about the court, and also came with her into her kitchen, and followed her mistress there also for … [a week] together, and that when she this informer did come into the said kitchen, the rat would be gone, but when her mistress was there alone, the rat would be about her, and that there was a good cat in the house, and yet he would not touch the said rat, although he were very near to him.'[35] It is plain that, in Gertrude's mind, this peculiarly bold and attentive rodent – which the household cat had wisely declined to tackle – was not, in fact, a rat at all, but was rather an evil spirit despatched by Stone to watch her victim and, if possible, to do her further harm.

The magistrates clearly took the claims made against Stone very seriously indeed, for she was ordered to appear at the next meeting of the sessions court. We must presume that she did so, but that she was either acquitted or let off with a relatively light punishment, for – while no documents relating to Stone's appearance in court appear to survive – in 1621 a female defendant in another case made passing reference to the fact that she had had sex with a man in a pig-stall 'in Mother Stones house' three weeks before.[36] It would seem that Stone escaped the capital penalty which had been imposed on Shorte and Wilkyns, then – and that she continued to live among her suspicious neighbours for some time to come.

Mary Stone was not the only Exeter woman to be reported to the JPs as a witch during the final years of James I's reign. In 1619, Mary Redwood, an expectant mother, came forward to testify that she had recently met a woman named Ann Heale in North Street, who had sworn 'that she [i.e. Ann] had bewitched her and prayed to God [that] she [i.e. Mary] might never be delivered of the child wherewith she goes until she had asked her forgiveness, for that she was the cause that she had been cucked'.[37] To be 'cucked' was to be strapped into the chair known as the 'cucking stool', and then repeatedly plunged under water: a punishment which was regularly handed out to disorderly persons in Exeter – and especially to scolds.[38] Ann had clearly blamed Mary for the fact that she herself had recently been humiliated in this way, then, and had threatened to gain her revenge through *maleficium*: yet another illustration of the way that scolding behaviour and allegations of witchery were so often linked in Tudor and Stuart Exeter. Yet, in the end, the JPs do not seem to have followed-up Mary's allegations, presumably because they considered the evidence too slight. Nor do they seem to have been unduly worried when they learned, in 1621, that a woman named Joanna Hurle had publically accused her neighbour, Elizabeth Burgess, of being a witch, and had declared that 'she did [be]witch ... [a] pig in Paris Street' (just outside East Gate). The fact that Joanna had gone on to call Elizabeth a 'whore' and to claim that 'she had three bastards', before knocking her opponent's head against a wall probably caused the JPs to disregard the allegation of witchcraft as just one more taunt in a torrent of all-purpose abuse.[39]

CHAPTER IV

The Reign of Charles I

In March 1625 James I died and was succeeded by his son,
Charles I. The new king was greatly influenced by his father,
and inherited many of his intellectual attitudes: including, it
would seem, a distinctly questioning approach to the subject
of witchcraft. During the last years of James's reign, successful
prosecutions for witchcraft in England had gone into a steep
decline, almost certainly because James had communicated his
own unease about the reliability of the evidence which was being
used to convict witches to the assize judges.[40] Once these senior
magistrates had become aware of the king's concerns, they
would inevitably have felt much more hesitant about pronouncing
sentence of death on any accused witches whose cases were
referred to them at the assizes. By the end of James's reign, in
other words, increasing royal scrupulousness about the quality
of evidence that was required in order to prosecute someone
successfully for witchcraft had made it far more difficult for local
accusers to secure the execution of suspected witches – and this
scrupulousness would continue to prevail during the reign of
his son.

Within months of the new king's accession, rumours of
witchcraft were again circulating in Exeter, and once again, those
rumours centred on Elizabeth Crosse: the blacksmith's wife who
had been denounced to the city JPs as a witch ten years before.

On that occasion, Richard and Margaret Patye had been prominent among Elizabeth's accusers, and the baker and his wife clearly believed that, over the intervening years, they had continued to suffer from her malign attentions. In June 1625 the Patyes re-appeared before the magistrates and unfolded a fresh tale of woe. Three or four years ago, Richard related, he had bought some sacks of corn in Exeter, loaded them onto his horse, and returned to his house in St Sidwells. There, Richard had begun to unload the sacks, 'his wife holding the horse by the head near the [hay]-stall'. But this scene of peaceful domesticity had been rudely shattered, Richard declared, when Elizabeth Crosse had suddenly appeared in the Patyes' yard and 'thrust in between the stall and his wife, and ... swore by the life of Christ that she would dwell in that house within this seven years'.[41]

Rallying swiftly, Margaret had retorted that, in order to fulfil her threat and take possession of their house, Crosse would need to 'witch away three lives'. This was presumably a reference to the fact that – as was common in Stuart Exeter – the Patyes' house was held on a lease which ran for the lives of three stated persons. It was not the happiest of rejoinders perhaps, and a few days later, Richard himself – who would surely have been one of the lessees – was given particular cause to remember it. He suddenly fell so seriously ill, he later assured the JPs, 'that he was like to die', and only recovered because he had the presence of mind to contact a certain Henry Rutley of Broadclyst – probably a 'cunning man', or healer, who was believed to possess skill in countering the enchantments of witches – who 'sent him some things whereby he was cured'.[42] Having told the story of his own narrow escape, Richard then returned to the subject of his pigs. He reminded the JPs that he believed that Crosse had killed many of his pigs in 1625, and declared that since then he had lost 80 more until 'he got help for them'. Clearly, Richard believed that Crosse had continued her occult campaign against his pigs until he had managed to procure some effective counter-charms.[43]

Margaret's story was more alarming still. She testified that, about four years since, she had gone out shopping in the city, and had been 'returning homewards again to her house in St Sidwells', when she had stopped, frozen in alarm, by the Little Conduit in the High Street. From her vantage point beside the fountain – which stood roughly where Castle Street meets High Street today – Margaret had spotted Elizabeth Crosse walking down the other side of the road in the opposite direction, having just come into the city from her own house in St Sidwells.[44] To Margaret's horror, Elizabeth now spotted her, too, and began to cross the street; it was plain that she meant to intercept the baker's wife. According to her later testimony, Margaret – who already believed her health to have suffered as a result of Crosse's enchantments – had previously been advised 'by some that had undertaken to cure her of [her] infirmities' – this was surely a reference to other 'cunning folk' – 'that … the next time she met her [i.e. Crosse] she should take the wall of her'.[45] The meaning of this phrase is a little ambiguous. On the one hand, Margaret's occult advisers may have been urging her to 'take the wall of' Elizabeth in a symbolic sense: or to stand up to her the next time that they met. On the other hand, they may have been advising her to 'take the wall' of Elizabeth in a literal sense: or to barge her physically off the pavement the next time that they encountered each other in the street and to force her into the road-way instead – conceivably because this manoeuvre was believed to somehow undermine a witch's power.

In the event, Margaret told the JPs, she had taken neither of these bold courses of action, because she had been far too frightened to do so. Instead, she had hidden herself in a nearby porch, 'where she [had] stayed so long as that the said Elizabeth might well have passed her by'. But Crosse was not to be shaken-off, for she, too, had 'made some delay and stop', Margaret went on, and had 'waited … [until] this informant came forth of the porch again'. And the moment she emerged from her hiding place, Margaret declared, her opponent had struck, like a snake, for 'the said Elizabeth met this informant full at the post of the porch, and went between the post and this informant, and gave this informant a thrust in the breast, so that … [she] have never since been able to give her children suck in that breast … and … says further that she went in great pain by reason [of that blow for] many days afterwards'.[46]

The Patyes were not the only witnesses to come forward against Crosse, for they were joined by John Wilton, a trainee apothecary, and two women named Elizabeth Beere and Sybilla Whitemore: all of whom had unsettling tales to tell about the blacksmith's formidable wife. Wilton told the magistrates that, after having brought two of his master's horses to be treated by John Crosse, he had had an argument with Elizabeth, whom he had accused of stealing some of the medicine which was intended for the animals. Elizabeth had reacted to this charge with fury, assuring the young apothecary that 'within this fortnight thou shall wish thou had not done it'. Ever since then, Wilton went on, he had not only felt unwell, but had also lost his professional skills, so that 'whatsoever he takes in hand, he cannot bring the same to any effects as formerly he has done, as namely for making of syrups [i.e. medicines] and letting of any one's blood, and he believes ... those things are fallen unto him by reason of ... Crosse his wife'. Beere, for her part, told the court that a friend of hers had recently told her that Elizabeth Crosse 'hath done her hurt, as she did think': perhaps because of a dispute over some apples. Whitemore's testimony was the most sinister of all. She told the magistrates that, after her husband and Elizabeth Crosse had fallen out two years ago, her husband, who – like Crosse's husband, was a smith – had suddenly found that he 'could not make any iron to work', while Whitemore family's had been struck by a mysterious illness so that 'there was nine of her household sick at one time, and she had one child was sick, and would eat so much as any three men could eat, and yet did consume in her body'.[47]

Having heard these vivid testimonies, the magistrates decided that Crosse had a clear case to answer, and she was bound over to appear at the next sessions, which were due to be held in July. Yet, even as the witnesses came forward to make their accusations against Crosse, plague was beginning to spread in Exeter and over the following weeks the disease ran rapidly out of control, spreading terror and fear across the entire city. Hundreds, if not thousands, of Exeter's inhabitants were to die in the epidemic and, during this time of terrible mortality, the normal court sittings were suspended. As a result, it was not until April 1626 that Crosse finally appeared at the Guildhall, and by this time, at least two of the witnesses against her – John Wilton and Sybilla Whitemore – were dead, having presumably died in the plague.[48]

Nevertheless, the Patyes were still very much alive – and determined to pursue their case. As a result, two indictments against Crosse were presented at the April sessions; one charging her with having bewitched Margaret and caused her to become gravely ill, the other with having bewitched Richard's pigs. Both of the indictments are endorsed '*a true bill*', showing that the grand jury had decided that the charges were credible ones and that the case should proceed to trial. Both of them are also endorsed '*not guilty*', however: showing either that the trial jury had been unconvinced by the evidence against Elizabeth, or that the judges had eventually decided that the case against her should be thrown out. The blacksmith's wife had foiled her accusers for a second time, then, and from this point onwards Elizabeth Crosse disappears from the historical record – though we know that her husband continued to ply his trade outside East Gate for many years to come.[49]

Elizabeth Crosse was not the only St Sidwells woman to possess an evil reputation during the early years of Charles I's reign, for in May 1627, so it was later alleged, 'Sith Coleman' – the wife of George Coleman, of St Sidwells, labourer – bewitched twenty pigs in that parish which belonged to a certain William Searle.[50] Three women and two men – one of them Searle himself – subsequently came forward to give evidence against the peculiarly named 'Sith', and an indictment against her was duly presented at the city sessions court. The grand jurors were clearly not convinced that the pigs' sufferings were attributable to witchcraft, however, and they dismissed the bill as *ignoramus*.[51] As a result, Coleman's wife was able to return home to St Sidwells, and its seems probable that she remained there for the rest of her days, for, in 1656, the parish clerk of St Sidwells recorded the burial of one 'Siefe Coleman': almost certainly the alleged 'witch' of thirty years before.[52]

In July 1627 fresh whispers of witchery reached the JPs, when two women from St Edmunds were reported to have spoken sinister words against Joseph Fill: a fuller (i.e. a cloth-worker) of the same parish. Thus Elizabeth Edie was said to have declared that 'she does hope that Joseph Fill shall kneel in his knees to her, and she will make him put his neck under … [her] foot', while Temperance Caselie was said to have boasted 'that she had voyte enough for Joseph Fill, and that she would have the body of him'.[53] Sadly, the precise meaning of the word 'voyte' remains obscure, but the two women's determination to humiliate Fill – and, in Caselie's case, to harm him in some mysterious and unspecified way, too – was made clear from their reported statements. Fill, for his part, had plainly believed that Caselie, Edie and a 25 year-old woman named Pentecost Edie – who was probably Elizabeth Edie's daughter – were all witches, for in March 1628 another witness appeared before the JPs to testify that, during the last summer, she had 'heard Joseph Fill say there were three strong witches in the lane … [namely] Pentecost Edie and Elizabeth Edie and Temperance Caselie and that Doctor Browne would take his oath for it'.[54]

These words are fascinating, not only because they show that Fill had publically declared three of the inhabitants of 'the lane' – by which he probably meant either Frog Lane or St Mary's Lane, just outside West Gate – to be witches, but also because they show that he had declared that a respected medical practitioner would be prepared to vouch for his accusations in court. As we shall see,

'Dr Browne' was to resurface in several subsequent witch-cases, and was clearly a learned 'cunning-man', who enjoyed a long-standing local reputation as an expert in occult affairs. The testimony of the woman who came forward in 1628 indicates that Fill had been signalling his intention to bring a formal prosecution for witchcraft against Caselie and the Edies, therefore: a prosecution which, he had boasted, would enjoy powerful expert support.

The first witness's testimony was backed up by that of a string of others, all of whom stated that both Fill and his wife, Joan, had regularly reviled Elizabeth Edie as a murderer and a witch. Thus a second witness testified that Joan Fill had often called Elizabeth Edie 'murderous jade, murderous rogue and murderous whore'.[55] A third confirmed that she had heard Joan describe Elizabeth as an 'old murderous whore', and threaten to 'make dice of her bones'. A fourth and fifth deposed that the Fills had insinuated that a local man, who had recently died, would still be alive were it not for Elizabeth. A sixth witness, finally, testified that, after Elizabeth had helped 'one Peter Judd's wife in childbirth' six months before, and the baby had died, 'this deponent heard the said Fill's wife say at Lightfoot's door that wheresoever the old jade was, she (meaning Elizabeth Edie) did rid [i.e. kill or destroy] one or other before she did return'.[56] We know that Peter Judd and Wilmot Ball had married in St Edmunds in 1623, and that their daughter, Joan, had been buried in August 1627.[57] Clearly, then, Joan Fill had assured at least one of her neighbours that Elizabeth Edie had been responsible for the baby girl's death.

Despite the flood of invective which the Fills had unleashed against the three alleged witches, there is no evidence to show that they managed to persuade anyone in authority to investigate the supposed occult activities of Caselie and the Edies. On the contrary, it appears to have been the Fills who aroused the JPs' displeasure in 1628 – presumably because they were disturbing the peace and vexing their neighbours – while the three women whom they had accused continued to live on in St Edmunds for some years to come.[58] That the justices responded to this bitter war of words in the way they did almost certainly reflects the fact that the Fills were a highly disputatious couple, while the Edies and Caselie enjoyed a good deal of local support – but it may also have been a sign that the Exeter JPs were by now adapting themselves to the changing political times.

During the 'Personal Rule' of 1629-40 – the period during which Charles I ruled England alone, without the assistance of parliaments – no witch-prosecutions appear to have taken place in Exeter; certainly no formal allegations of witchcraft are recorded in the relevant order books of the city court.[59] The cessation of judicial activity against witches at Exeter during the 1630s almost certainly reflected the fact that, at the national level, too, the prosecution of witches was in steep decline. In 1634, Charles had personally intervened in a witch-trial in Lancashire and it had emerged that the evidence of the leading witness was a tissue of lies.[60] In the wake of this case, assize judges had become more unwilling than ever to convict accused witches – and during the late 1630s, only two or three witches are known to have been executed across the whole of England.[61]

Because belief in witchcraft remained near-universal at this time, many of Charles's subjects may well have felt distinctly uneasy about the direction of royal policy when it came to the

prosecution – or non-prosecution – of witches. In the absence of
Parliament, there was no one to whom they could complain. But,
by the end of the 1630s, Charles was facing growing opposition
to his religious and financial policies: particularly among the
most zealous Protestants, or 'puritans'. In 1640 he was forced to
summon a Parliament and, after relations between the king and
his critics in the House of Commons finally collapsed, in 1642,
a full-scale Civil War between Royalists and Parliamentarians
broke out across the entire country. Exeter's ruling council
had long been dominated by a powerful puritan faction and in
mid-1642 these men succeeded in manoeuvring the city into
the Parliamentarian camp.[62] It was a revolution in local affairs –
and it was one which would influence official attitudes towards
witchcraft in Exeter, just as it would influence everything else.

CHAPTER V

The Rule of Parliament

By late 1642, Parliament's supporters controlled Devon while
Charles I's supporters controlled Cornwall. In November, fierce
fighting broke out between the two sides and in December a
Cornish Royalist army advanced upon Exeter with the aim of
recapturing the city for the king. No sooner had the Cornish
troops arrived before Exeter, however, than they heard that a
powerful Parliamentarian army was marching down to the city's
relief – so they hastily abandoned their siege. The Royalists'
retreat prompted general rejoicing among Parliament's puritanical
supporters in Exeter, who celebrated their deliverance by
smashing up the ornate furniture and fittings of the Cathedral
– which they regarded as quasi-Catholic – and by fining and
imprisoning many of the king's local sympathisers.[63] It seems
unlikely to be coincidence that it was during this carnival of anti-
Royalist activity in Exeter – a carnival which marked the open
rejection of the king's authority by the citizens – that allegations of
witchcraft again began to be seriously investigated by the city JPs:
for the first time, so far as we can tell, since the dismissal of the
case against Sith Coleman some fourteen years before.

On 28 December Anne King, the wife of William King – a
weaver of St Mary Major parish – was accused of attempting to find
lost goods through witchcraft.[64] The examining magistrate clearly
felt that there was a case to answer for, in January 1643, Anne was

bound over to appear at the next sessions.[65] With a Parliamentarian regime now firmly established in Exeter – and with the city's puritan magistrates no longer obliged to defer to royal scruples about the legal sufficiency of the evidence produced in witch-prosecutions – more such cases could easily have followed. Yet the fortunes of war were about to turn against the Parliamentarians and in September 1643 Exeter was captured by the Royalists. With the king's authority restored – and with the more zealously puritan JPs having withdrawn from local affairs – no further witch-prosecutions are known to have occurred in Exeter over the next three years.

The Royalist triumph in the West was to prove short-lived. In late 1645, Parliament's New Model Army swept through Dorset and Somerset and advanced to the very gates of Exeter. The king's troops within the city were determined to resist, and, as a result, Exeter suffered a long siege during the winter of 1645-46: a siege which resulted in most of the city suburbs – including most of Holy Trinity parish and the whole of St Sidwells – being razed to the ground.[66] By the time the Royalists finally agreed to surrender, in April 1646, Exeter was a battered shadow of its former self, and the Royalist cause across the entire country was on its knees. Charles I surrendered himself to his enemies just a few months later, with the result that the kingdom was now ruled by the victorious Parliamentarians, rather than by the king. With Parliament firmly back in control of Exeter, its local supporters now resumed the direction of civic affairs – and it is interesting to note that, within less than a year, a fresh case of witchcraft was brought to the attention of the city magistrates. In November 1646 John Lendon, carpenter, was reported 'for witchcraft, for taking of money and [for] telling where things lost are to be found'.[67]

Lendon cannot have been punished too harshly, as his name was to crop up again in the sessions records five years later.[68] Nevertheless, anyone accused of witchcraft in England in 1646 would have had good reason to feel thoroughly alarmed. In East Anglia and parts of the South-East, a full scale witch-hunt was by now in progress, under the direction of Matthew Hopkins: the so-called 'Witch-Finder General'. Some 100 people were executed between 1645 and 1647 as a direct result of the atmosphere of terror which Hopkins and his allies had managed to stoke-up, and, although Exeter was a long way from the epicentre of the panic, there can be little doubt that the townsfolk would have been well aware of the devilish goings-on up-country.[69] In the event, no-one apart from Lendon is known to have been denounced to the city JPs as a witch during the late 1640s and – thanks to a widespread perception among leading Parliamentarians that 'witch-hunting' had got out of hand during 1645-47 – the tempo of witch prosecutions across the country as a whole began to slacken thereafter. Nevertheless, a considerable number of executions for witchcraft continued to occur after the beheading of Charles I and the establishment of the English Republic in 1649 – and Exeter was to see a rash of witch-prosecutions during the 1650s.[70]

The first came in November 1652 when Grace Matthews, the wife of Nicholas Matthews, labourer, came forward to testify to the magistrates. About three years ago, Grace stated, her husband had been 'taken sick and supposed to have been bewitched'. Grace had therefore hurried to see 'Doctor Browne': evidently the same man whom Joseph Fill had consulted about the supposed witches of St Edmunds in 1627. Browne had initially given Grace some medicine, but this had done her husband 'little good'. Disappointed, Grace had gone back to Browne to ask him if there was nothing more he could do, at which point he had cautiously acknowledged 'that he could formerly do something to cure people that had been bewitched'. This was a curious turn of phrase, which hinted that – knowing that 'cunning folk' could all too easily be accused of witchcraft themselves – Browne was somewhat hesitant about openly confessing to his supposed powers. Nevertheless, he had shown that he was prepared to help Grace in a roundabout way, for he had advised her to 'go to a woman in Broadclyst who was sometime his servant for that purpose'.[71]

Having gone to Broadclyst to consult this woman, Grace had, once again, been supplied with 'some remedies … for her … husband'. Medicines were clearly not all that 'the woman of Broadclyst' was in the habit of dispensing, however, for she had also given Grace some alarming advice, warning her 'that she should be very wary of a woman living near unto her who was tall of stature, of a pale face, a blinking eye, and using to go by a staff when she did come to her house'. (This was, of course, a very good summing-up of just what many contemporaries expected a malefic witch to look like.) Browne's former servant had then gone on to stress that, if a woman answering this description were to come to Grace's house, she should 'give her nothing', for - so the 'cunning woman' assured poor Grace – 'her … husband was [already] bewitched, and … the plot was laid for herself [too]'. With these terrifying words still ringing in her ears, Grace had returned to Exeter.[72]

That night, as she was 'washing her … [sick] husband's body', Grace had heard a knock at the door, and, upon going to answer it, had found herself confronted by 'Joan, the wife of John Baker ... butcher', who had told Grace that she wished 'to buy some commodities of her'. Clearly suspecting that Baker was the witch whom she had been warned against earlier that day, Grace had refused to enter into any sort of transaction with her, and had sent Baker packing. Yet, soon afterwards, Baker had returned – this time while Grace was away from the house – and had managed to persuade the Matthews' maid-servant to sell her some things, 'for which she ... paid her three pence'. The result of this fatal exchange, Grace went on to imply, was almost exactly what the cunning woman had foretold, for, shortly afterwards, 'her ... servant fell sick also, lying for the space of three quarters of a year in a languishing condition, being altogether pined and consumed away in her body, and so died ... [as a result of witchcraft] as she verily believeth, for that her ... servant often cried out in her sickness that she was bewitched'.[73]

A second witness then appeared before the magistrates to give further evidence against Joan Baker. This man deposed that, having gone to visit Baker's husband the night before, he had 'come into a room of the said Baker's house ... [and] found ... Baker's wife sitting by the fire and there saw her to have a toad in her lap, and two more at her feet'.[74] That Joan Baker should have enjoyed the intimate companionship of toads would have been regarded by many contemporaries as highly suspicious. As we have seen, John Walsh had declared as long ago as 1566 that the familiar spirits nurtured by West Country witches commonly assumed the shape of toads, while during James I's reign, one Exeter man had cursed a woman as 'a witch and toad' and another had roundly abused his own wife in precisely the same terms –

clearly suggesting that witches and toads continued to be closely linked in the popular imagination.[75] Just a year before Baker was denounced to the JPs, moreover, a third Exeter man had called his mother 'witch and toad', while, just a few years *after* this, a fourth was to term a woman of St Sidwells 'witch', and to declare that 'she kept a pot of toads in her house'.[76] To claim that Baker consorted with toads was to suggest something very sinister indeed, then – and the JPs promptly ordered that she should be committed to the gaol.[77]

What happened immediately after this is unclear, but in September 1653, Grace Matthews and three other witnesses were ordered to appear at the next sessions to give evidence against Joan Baker 'on suspicion of murder for witchcraft'. At the same time, a fourth witness – formerly a servant to a city brewer – came forward to testify to the JPs. He told them that, four years ago, Baker had 'come to … his then master's house to beg a little yeast … unto whom this informant said he would give her none … whereunto the said Joan Baker replied that there was yeast enough in the cellar'. After this uncomfortable exchange, the witness went on, 'for a fortnight together there was little or no yeast would come off from the beer then brewed'. As a result of these repeated failures in the brewing process, the witness concluded, indignantly, he had been dismissed from his master's service, but, as soon as another man was taken on in his place, 'the yeast did usually come off from the working of the drink, as in the past it did do'. He, too, was promptly bound over to appear at the next sessions.[78]

Sadly, the outcome of the legal proceedings which had been instigated against Joan Baker is unknown, but it was not long before another Exeter woman would find herself hauled before the magistrates as a suspected witch. Diana Crosse, widow, was a former resident of Holy Trinity parish. Before the Civil War, she had kept some sort of 'school' at Magdalen Hill Head, but – following the destruction of the city suburbs by the Royalists in 1645-46 – she, like all of her neighbours, had been forced to find shelter elsewhere. How Crosse managed to survive in the wake of this disaster, and where she went next, we do not know, but by the early 1650s she was living in St Mary Major parish, within the city walls. Here, in either late 1653 or early 1654, she was arrested and formally accused of witchcraft, before being tried at the city court. In April 1654 it was noted by the clerk of that court that Crosse had recently been 'indicted for practising witchcraft upon the person of … Joan Poole, wife of John Poole … glover' but that the indictment had been dismissed as *ignoramus* by the grand jurors.[79]

Crosse must have hoped that this would mark the end of her troubles, but the magistrates clearly believed that she had other charges to answer. They ordered the unfortunate widow to appear at the next sessions, and 'in the meanwhile to be of good behaviour'.[80] Then, in July, six witnesses came forward to deliver a string of fresh testimonies against Crosse.[81] Among them was Anne Southcott, who deposed that, before the war, she had been one of Crosse's neighbours, and had sent 'a girl of hers to school with the foresaid … Crosse' for the space of a year. Anne had then decided to remove her child from 'that school' and to 'put it to school again to one goodwife Woodman, a near neighbour to this informant'. This was to prove a fatal error, Anne went on to allege, for 'in a very short time thereafter the said child became sick and lay in a languishing condition for 5 years together, and

then died'. Nor was this all, she declared, for 'five weeks after the
... child died, her ... first husband died also, and ... about seven
weeks thereafter ... Woodman, the child's second school-mistress,
died likewise'. Anne was confident that these misfortunes were
the result of bewitchment, she told the JPs, because 'in the time of
her said child's sickness, she went to one Mrs Mannowaye, whose
husband was a doctor of physic, for some physical remedies
for her ... child ... [and] the said Mrs Mannowaye willed this
informant to go home and have a care of her child, saying withal
that it was a dying child, and that she lived by a bad neighbour'.[82]

The testimony of the other witnesses made it clear that Crosse
had fallen on hard times since her days in Holy Trinity – and that
she had long possessed a local reputation as a witch. Jane Dicker,
for example, informed the court that, two years ago, Crosse had
come 'to her husband's house to beg some relief'. After Dicker had
told Crosse that she had nothing to give – and had added insult
to injury by 'calling her old witch' – Crosse had then replied 'that
it had been better she had given her something'. Soon after this,
Dicker alleged, 'a child of hers fell sick, and in cleansing her house
she found a toad in her chamber'.[83] Again, we see the suggestion
here that local witches were in the habit of sending demons in the
shape of toads to strike down their victims.

Emlyn Poe, a cloth-maker's wife, similarly claimed that a
refusal to grant charity to Diana Crosse had been followed by
sudden misfortune. She informed the court that, some months
ago, Crosse 'came unto her house for a little drink, which this
informant gave her', but that when Crosse returned 'a second
and third time afterwards, she ... refused to give her any [more]'.
Shortly after Crosse's last visit, two of Poe's children 'fell sick'. Not

was this all, Poe went on, for about two years ago, her husband had also fallen ill, 'complaining that he was much pained and grieved in his limbs'. Worried by her husband's strange symptoms, Poe had gone to see the ubiquitous Dr Browne to ask him 'for some remedy and directions to be given … for her husband's recovery'. Browne had, once again, responded in a distinctly cagey fashion, telling Poe 'that he could not give her any [help], but wished her to go home and give her husband some hot broth … [adding] that he should be wary and have a care another time'. Poe evidently took this gnomic utterance to mean that Browne believed her husband to have been bewitched – and later concluded that Crosse was the culprit. This conclusion can only have been reinforced when some of Poe's neighbours told her that they had seen Crosse in her house, and 'her chimney in a very short time afterwards … [caught] fire, there being then little or no fire in the hearth'.[84]

Some of the most disturbing testimony against Crosse was provided by Mary Cleake, the sister of Joan Poole: the sick woman whom Crosse had been accused – and cleared – of bewitching at her previous trial. Cleake testified that Crosse had recently been 'brought down' to the Magdalen Almshouses outside South Gate – by whom, and for what specific purpose she does not state – where her sister was then 'kept, being in a sad and distracted condition'. No sooner had Joan Poole spotted Crosse, Cleake deposed, than she had flown into a violent rage, and 'fell presently upon the said … Crosse, and, beating of her, cried out that she was her adversary'. Cleake clearly regarded her sister's violent outburst as proof that she knew that Crosse was her occult tormentor. Cleake then went on to declare that she herself had attempted to break the power of Crosse's supposed enchantments, but that, although she had pricked Crosse with a needle '12 several times … to draw some blood from her, yet [she] could not fetch any blood from her, the said Crosse nothing grudging thereat'.[85] Here we see evidence of the contemporary belief that one of the sure marks of a witch was the presence on his or her body of places which did not bleed when 'pricked' and were insensible to pain.[86]

Henry Hernaman, who was one of Exeter's 'sergeants at mace' – the civic officials who attended upon the mayor – also came forward to testify against Crosse. He deposed that, soon after she had been acquitted at her previous trial, Crosse had 'come to the council chamber door' in the Guildhall, 'with a petition in her hand, desiring this informant to carry it in to Mr Mayor'. It would be fascinating to know what was in Crosse's petition – and whether, being a former 'schoolmistress', she had drawn it up herself. All we can say for sure is that Hernaman turned a deaf ear to Crosse's request. He had refused to deliver her petition to the mayor, he told the JPs – and, just a week later, 'his wife was taken sick and complained much in her limbs', while 'a boy of his in the same week fell and broke his arm'.[87] Like all the other witnesses, Hernaman clearly believed that his misfortunes were a direct result of his refusal to help Diana Crosse.

A month after these testimonies had been made, Crosse's case was considered at the summer assizes. No final decision appears to have been reached, however, for in late August, the clerk of the city court noted that 'by order of the judge at the last assizes, Diana Crosse … is delivered unto bail to appear at the next sessions'.[88] Over the following months, preparations were made for a new trial, and in January 1655 Crosse re-appeared before the city court on a fresh charge of witchcraft. This time the indictment against her was declared a true bill, so the case proceeded to trial – but Crosse was then found 'not guilty' by the trial jury. As a result, the proceedings against her collapsed yet again, but, for whatever reason, the JPs still did not feel that they could allow her to walk free. On 8 January, it was recorded that 'Diana Crosse ... being at this sessions indicted for a witch, but acquitted by the petty jury is ordered to be kept in the gaol'.[89] What became of Crosse next, and whether she ever managed to escape from the legal toils into which she had fallen remains, for the moment, unclear.

Further witch-prosecutions continued to disturb the peace of the city throughout the next five years. In 1656, for example, Elizabeth Babbage, of St Thomas, widow, was indicted on a charge of having bewitched to death Margery Stone: the daughter of a barber from St Olaves.[90] In 1658, Ambrose Cole, a surgeon of St Thomas, was ordered to appear at the next sessions to reply to accusations that he, too, was 'a conjuror or witch'.[91] Then, in August that year, Elizabeth Lowton, the wife of Ralph Lowton of St George's parish, came forward to accuse a woman of bewitching her daughter, Jane. Elizabeth informed the JPs that Jane had recently suffered from 'dangerous fits in all parts of her body', sometimes lasting for two hours at a time. During the course of these episodes, Elizabeth stated, she had hardly been able to hold Jane down in her bed, 'she lying in a manner speechless'. Yet what had made these seizures even more terrifying, Elizabeth told the JPs, was the fact that 'in the beginning ... of her fits her said daughter did relate unto her that she did see a woman standing before her with a firebrand in her hand, her ... daughter stamping with her feet and stirring with her arms and hands ... and offering to strike at the woman in a way of defiance'.[92]

Almost out of her wits with worry, Elizabeth had gone to
consult yet another cunning man: this time, one 'George Roch,
late a prisoner in the High Gaol'. (As we have seen, this was the
common prison for the county of Devon, which lay just off Castle
Lane, in the shadow of Exeter Castle.) Roch had confirmed that
Jane's illness was, indeed, an unnatural one, and had told Elizabeth
'that her … daughter was bewitched by a woman' who dwelt
under the Lowtons' own roof. Elizabeth had at once identified
this woman as Joan, the wife of John Taylor, yeoman, who lived
in her house, presumably as a tenant. With the culprit identified,
Roch had then urged Elizabeth to take heart, for 'he did hope
to cure her said daughter without any outward means, only by
looking into a book and giving her a ticket [probably a slip of
paper with charms written on it] to hang about her neck'. And
sure enough, Elizabeth told the JPs, Roch's counter-charms had
proved to be so efficacious 'that since that time her daughter has
not been troubled with any fit at all'.[93]

Jane herself now appeared to testify to the truth of her
mother's story, telling the JPs that 'in the midst of her fits, she
plainly saw the foresaid Joan Taylor to stand before her with
a firebrand in her hand, offering to throw it at her, there then
appearing others in the shape of men and women'. Who these
'others' were Jane did not say, but her phraseology hints that she
believed them to be evil spirits or demons. The JPs were evidently
convinced by the Lowtons' claims, for that very day Taylor was
bound over to appear at the next sessions.[94] As a yeoman's wife,
Joan Taylor is the most socially elevated woman who is known
to have been formally presented as a witch at the Exeter sessions
between 1563 and 1660. It is possible that her relatively high

social status may have acted in her favour, for, when Taylor's case at last came to trial before the city court – in January 1659 – the indictment against her was declared to be 'no true bill' and she was acquitted.[95]

In January 1659 Agnes Green, a weaver's wife, came forward to make fresh allegations of witchcraft to the JPs. She testified that, for six weeks past, her husband, Humphrey, had been 'often taken with fits in his head and other distempers in his body', and declared that she was sure that he had been bewitched.[96] Humphrey's tormentor, Agnes believed, was a widow from Holy Trinity parish named Joan Furnace. Whenever Furnace came to see her husband, Agnes reported, he appeared to be well, 'but as soon as she is gone out of his sight [he] falls into the like distracted condition again.'[97] Why Furnace should have been visiting Humphrey in the first place Agnes did not say, but it seems probable that the widow had originally been invited to the afflicted man's bedside because she, too, possessed a reputation as a 'cunning woman'. Elsewhere in her testimony, Agnes mentioned that, when one of her children had previously fallen sick, 'the same Joan Furnace came to her and told her that her child was creemed with [i.e. squeezed by] the fairies.'[98] As we have seen, cunning folk were thought to be able to counter the harm done by malevolent fairies, so it is possible that Furnace had originally been asked to examine the child in the hope she might be able to help it. Agnes concluded her testimony, moreover, by deposing that, since that time, Furnace had 'touched another child of hers with her hand on the forehead [and] the child presently had its forehead covered over with sores' – a statement which, again, hints at the possibility that an initial attempt to cure the child by the 'laying on of hands' had later come to be seen as a deliberate attempt to do it harm.[99] In the wake of Agnes's testimony, Furnace was formally charged with witchcraft at the city court a few days later but was found not guilty by the trial jury.[100]

CHAPTER VI

After 1660

By the time Joan Furnace appeared before the Exeter magistrates, Oliver Cromwell was dead, and the English republic was crumbling. Within months, the monarchy was on the point of being restored and in May 1660 Charles I's eldest son was proclaimed throughout the country as King Charles II. The Restoration heralded another crucial shift in the history of English witchcraft. Perhaps because the new king shared the sceptical attitude of his father and grandfather, perhaps because the puritans had now fallen from power, perhaps because opinion among the English social and judicial elite as a whole was now moving towards the view that, while witchcraft might exist, it was almost impossible to prove it, the number of witch-prosecutions across the country as a whole went into rapid decline after 1660.[101] Yet this change did not happen overnight – or at least not in Exeter – and in July 1660 a widow named Bridget Wotton was reported to the JPs as a witch. Wotton, like other Exonians accused of witchcraft before her, was said to have used toads to harm her neighbours. Some twelve years ago, it was claimed, she had cast a toad into a pig's trough belonging to a woman in North Street, 'and immediately her pig, then feeding at the trough, was taken mad … tumbling up and down on his head from the said house to North Gate and died'. Not only this, Wotton was said to have brought a toad into another house in North Street, with the

54

result that a woman dwelling there had been 'taken in a very sad condition'. In addition, Wotton was alleged to have bewitched a third woman so that she became 'extreme sick' – and the afflicted woman herself appeared before the JPs to testify that, while she had been lying ill in bed, both in her mother's house in St Paul's parish and in her husband's house in St Davids, she had seen 'the person or shape of the said Bridget' in a corner of her bed-chamber.[102]

The testimonies given against Wotton – and the fact that, once the JPs had heard them, she was bound over to appear at the next sessions – make it clear that there were still powerful currents of opinion in post-Restoration Exeter which advocated the prosecution of witchcraft.[103] It is possible, indeed, that Exeter's deep-rooted tradition of popular witch-belief may do something to explain why the city was the last place in England to see people hanged for the alleged crime of witchcraft. By the final years of Charles II's reign, it had become standard practice for assize judges confronted with witchcraft cases to either steer trial juries away from delivering a guilty verdict, or, if this tactic failed, to grant the accused witch a reprieve. In 1683, however, three North Devon women were found guilty of witchcraft at the Devon assizes held at Exeter Castle – and subsequently hanged. In several subsequent accounts of this affair, one of the judges who had been present at the assizes – Sir Francis North – and his brother, Roger, sought to explain why the trial judge, Sir Thomas Raymond, had come to the decision that he had. Both of them implied that popular pressure had played its part, and that Raymond had feared that, if he allowed the witches to escape, there would be an explosion of rage among local people: one which might be

exploited, in its turn, by the 'faction', that is to say, by puritan
or nonconformist critics of the Crown.[104] Roger, in particular,
claimed that the three women had been 'brought to the assizes [at
the Castle] with as much noise and fury of the rabble against them
as could be showed on any occasion'.[105] While some – perhaps
the majority – of those who made up this intimidating 'rabble'
were clearly from the surrounding countryside, it is hard to doubt
that there were many Exeter people among them, too. Exonians
almost certainly contributed to the popular clamour which helped
to bring about the last witch executions in England, therefore,
and even after the witchcraft acts had finally been repealed, in
1736, voices continued to be raised against 'witches' in the city for
decades to come.

As late as 1837, indeed, one young Exeter woman, Mary Anne
Shapland, openly accused another, Mary Anne Dymond, of being
a shape-shifting witch in the same Guildhall court-room in which
so many alleged witches had been prosecuted during the Tudor
and Stuart periods. Shapland initially complained to the justices
that Dymond had assaulted her. Dymond responded to this by
launching a counter-charge of her own, stating that, over the past
few months, 'this female has annoyed me in the streets very much
and accused me of being a witch'. Dymond went on to complain
that Shapland had sought to draw a enchanted circle around her
door 'so that I should not witch her any more'; had accused her
of coming into her room at night in the shape of a cat; and had
'asked me if I would allow her to prick my thumb with a needle,
as the slightest prick that would draw blood would spoil my work'.
Upon being asked by the mayor if she really believed Dymond to
be a witch, Shapland 'after some hesitation admitted that she did',

and went on to accuse Dymond both of keeping a toad and of infesting her body with lice. At the dawn of the railway age, these claims were met with amused disbelief by the city magistrates – who eventually agreed to fine Dymond a shilling for taking advantage of Shapland's 'credulity' before dismissing the case – but just 200 years before, precisely the same claims, made in precisely the same setting, could well have led to a tragedy.[106] Viewed from one angle, in other words, the case of Shapland versus Dymond demonstrates just how much attitudes towards witchcraft had changed in Exeter between the accession of Queen Elizabeth I and the accession of Queen Victoria, but, viewed from another, it hints at just how much they had remained stubbornly, persistently the same.[107]

Persons denounced to the Exeter JPs as witches between 1558 and 1660

1558 April: **Thomas Weare** [1] presented by the city law jury as 'a charmer & a wytchecrafte user'.[108] He was subsequently banished from Exeter.

1559 October: **Frauncys Dyrym** [2] presented by the city law jury 'for her suspected witchcraft'.[109] She was subsequently banished from Exeter.

1565 October: **Matilda Parke** [3], wife of Roger Parke (of Holy Trinity), apprehended on suspicion of using 'arte magice'. Indicted, pleaded not guilty, found guilty.[110] She was subsequently banished from Exeter.

1566 April: **Alice Meade** [4] of Exmouth, widow, and Maud Parke (see above) arraigned for witchcraft.[111] Indicted, pleaded not guilty, both found guilty.[112] Outcome unknown – both hanged?

1581 April: Three indictments for witchcraft presented against **Thomasine Shorte** [5], wife of Robert Shorte, of St Sidwells.[113] All found to be true bills. She was found guilty and hanged.

1600 March: One indictment presented against **Richard Wilkyns** [6], of Holy Trinity, labourer.[114] Outcome unknown, but Wilkyns clearly survived.

1602 April: Three indictments presented against **Joanna Brice [7]**, wife of William Brice of St Sidwells, labourer.[115] All found to be true bills. She was condemned to death, but subsequently reprieved.

1610 July: Eight indictments presented against Richard Wilkyns.[116] All but one found to be true bills. He was found guilty and executed.

1615 July: Three indictments presented against **John Crosse [8]** of St Sidwell's, blacksmith, and **Elizabeth Crosse [9]** his wife.[117] Two were declared to be 'ignoramus', but one, relating specifically to Elizabeth, was not. She was tried, but eventually, it would seem, acquitted.

1619 July: witness informs the city magistrates that **Ann Heale [10]** is a witch.[118] No further action known to have been taken.

1620 August: magistrates informed that **Mary Stone [11]** of Exeter, widow, is a witch. Six depositions taken; three witnesses ordered to give further testimony against Stone at the next sessions.[119] The outcome of the case is unknown.

1626 April: two indictments presented against Elizabeth Crosse.[120] Both found to be true bills, but Crosse found not guilty.

1627 April: one indictment presented against **Sith Coleman [12]**, wife of George Coleman, of St Sidwells, labourer.[121] The indictment was declared ignoramus, and Coleman appears to have lived on into the 1650s.

1642 December: **Anna King [13]**, wife of William King, of St Mary Major accused of witchcraft and bound over to appear at the next sessions.[122] The outcome is unknown, but it would appear that King was still alive in 1656.

1646   November: **John Lendon [14]** of Exeter (St Mary Major), carpenter, reported to one of the JPs for witchcraft.[123] The outcome of the case is unknown, but Lendon was clearly still alive in the 1650s.

1652   November: **Joan Baker [15]**, wife of John Baker, of Exeter, butcher, committed to prison as a suspected witch.[124] In September 1653, several witnesses were bound over to give evidence against her at the next sessions. The outcome of the case is unknown.

1654   April: Indictment presented against **Diana Crosse [16]** of St Mary Major, widow.[125] The indictment was declared ignoramus, but Crosse was bound over to appear at the next sessions. Further proceedings against Crosse took place throughout 1654, and towards the end of that year, a further indictment was drawn up against her.[126] This was found to be a true bill, but Crosse was acquitted by the trial jury in January 1655. What happened to her next is unknown.

1656   July: Indictment presented against **Elizabeth Babbage [17]**, of St Thomas, widow.[127] Found to be a true bill. The outcome of the case is unknown.

1658   July: **Ambrose Cole [18]** of St Thomas, surgeon, bound over to appear at the next sessions as a suspected witch.[128] He duly appeared at the next sessions and was discharged. **Joan Taylor [19]**, wife of John Taylor, yeoman, of St George's parish, accused of witchcraft.[129] An indictment was presented against her at the Christmas 1658 sessions, but was declared no true bill.[130]

1659   January: **Joan Furnace [20]** of Holy Trinity, widow, accused of witchcraft.[131] A formal indictment was presented against her at the January 1659 sessions, but she was found not guilty.[132]

1660   July: **Bridget Wotton [21]** of Exeter, widow, bound over to the next sessions as a suspected witch.[133] The outcome of this case is unknown.

November: **Katherine Bright [22]**, widow and **Edward Bright [23]**, cordwainer, of South Tawton, in Devon, bound over to the next Devon County Assizes as suspected witches.[134]

Total number of accused witches:

23 (6 men and 17 women)

Total number of indictments: 29

Places of residence of suspected witches:

Exeter, parish unknown:	6
Exeter, St Sidwells:	5
Exeter, Holy Trinity:	3
Exeter, St Mary Major:	3
Exeter, St George:	1
Devon, Exmouth:	1
Devon: St Thomas:	2
Devon: South Tawton:	2
Total:	**23**

Occupations of suspected witches:

Wives:	8
Widows:	7
Unknown:	3
Blacksmith;	1
Carpenter:	1
Cordwainer:	1
Labourer:	1
Surgeon:	1
Total:	**23**

Select Bibliography of secondary sources cited in the text

J. Barry, *Witchcraft and Demonology in South West England, 1640-1789* (Basingstoke, 2012).

M. Braddick, *God's Fury, England's Fire: A New History of the English Civil Wars* (London, 2008).

J.S. Cockburn, *A History of English Assizes, 1558–1714* (Cambridge, 1972).

W. Cotton and H. Woolcombe, *Gleanings from the Municipal and Cathedral Records of Exeter* (Exeter, 1877).

O. Davies, *A People Bewitched: Witchcraft and Magic in Nineteenth-Century Somerset* (Trowbridge, 1999).

G. Durston, *Witchcraft and Witch Trials: A History of English Witchcraft and its Legal Perspectives, 1542-1736* (Chichester, 2000).

M. Gaskill, *Witchfinders: A Seventeenth-Century English Tragedy* (London, 2005).

T. Gray and J. Draisey, 'Witchcraft in the Diocese of Exeter, Part III', *Devon and Cornwall Notes and Queries* [hereafter: *DCNQ*], volume 36, part 9 (spring, 1991).

T. Gray, *Strumpets and Ninnycocks: Name-Calling in Devon, 1540-1640* (Exeter, 2016).

C.G. Henderson, 'The Development of the South Gate of Exeter and its Role in the City Defences', *Proceedings of the Devon Archaeological Society*, 59 (2001).

W.G. Hoskins, 'The Elizabethan Merchants of Exeter', in P. Clark (ed.), *The Early Modern Town: A Reader* (London, 1976).

C. L'Estrange-Ewen, *Witch-Hunting and Witch Trials* (New York, 1929).

P.G. Maxwell-Stuart, *The British Witch: The Biography* (Stroud, 2014).

J. Sharpe, *Instruments of Darkness: Witchcraft in England, 1550-1750* (London, 1996).

J. Sharpe, *Witchcraft in Early Modern England* (London, 2001).

M. Stoyle, 'Whole Streets Converted to Ashes: Property Destruction in Exeter during the English Civil War', *Southern History,* 16 (1994).

M. Stoyle, *From Deliverance to Destruction: Rebellion and Civil War in an English City* (Exeter, 1996).

M. Stoyle, 'Two New Seventeenth Century Witch Cases from Exeter', *DCNQ*, volume 40, part 6 (autumn, 2009).

M. Stoyle, 'The Execution of a Witch in Elizabethan Exeter', *DCNQ*, volume 40, part 7 (spring, 2010).

M. Stoyle, 'It is but an Old Witch Gone: Prosecution and Execution for Witchcraft in Exeter, 1558-1610', *History*, 96, number 322 (April, 2011).

M. Stoyle, 'Witchcraft in Exeter: The Case of the Widow Stone, 1619-20', *DCNQ*, volume 40, part 9 (spring, 2011).

M. Stoyle, *Water in the City: The Aqueducts and Underground Passages of Exeter* (Exeter, 2014).

M. Stoyle, 'Witchcraft in Exeter: The Cases of John and Elizabeth Crosse', *DCNQ*, volume 41, part 7 (spring, 2015).

K. Thomas, *Religion and the Decline of Magic: Studies in Popular Belief in Sixteenth- and Seventeenth-Century England* (1971; London, 1997 edition).

J. Thompson, *Wives, Widows, Witches and Bitches: Women in Seventeenth- Century Devon* (New York, 1993).

D. Underdown, 'The Taming of the Scold: The Enforcement of Patriarchal Authority in early modern England', in A. Fletcher and J. Stevenson (eds), *Order and Disorder in Early Modern England* (Cambridge, 1985).

E. Wilby, *Cunning Folk and Familiar Spirits: Shamanistic Visionary Traditions in Early Modern British Witchcraft and Magic* (Eastbourne, 2010).

T. Wright, 'The Municipal Archives of Exeter', *Journal of British Archaeology*, volume 18 (1862)

Notes

[1]   T. Wright, 'The Municipal Archives of Exeter', *Journal of British Archaeology*, volume 18 (1862), p. 307.

[2]   J. Sharpe, *Instruments of Darkness: Witchcraft in England, 1550-1750* (1996), p. 121. For the most recent account of the trial of 'the Bideford witches' in 1683, see J. Barry, *Witchcraft and Demonology in South-West England, 1640-1789* (Basingstoke, 2012), pp. 58-102.

[3]   For the city's population in the 1550s, see W.G. Hoskins, 'The Elizabethan Merchants of Exeter', in P. Clark (ed.), *The Early Modern Town: A Reader* (1976), p. 149.

[4]   J. and J.H. Wylie (eds), *Report on the Records of the City of Exeter*, Historical Manuscripts Commission (1916), p. 5.

[5]   C.G. Henderson, 'The Development of the South Gate of Exeter and its Role in the City Defences', *Proceedings of the Devon Archaeological Society*, 59 (2001), pp. 103-08; and W.J. Harte and others (eds), A *Description of the City of Exeter, by John Vowell, Alias Hooker: Part II* (Devon and Cornwall Record Society, 1919), p. 359.

[6]   T. Gray (ed.), *The Chronicle of Exeter, 1205-1722* (Exeter, 2005), p. 74.

[7]   Sharpe, *Instruments*, pp. 27-29.

[8]   Devon Heritage Centre, Exeter [hereafter: DHC], Exeter City Archives [hereafter: ECA], Book 100, f. 22.

[9]   T. Gray and J. Draisey, 'Witchcraft in the Diocese of Exeter, Part III, *Devon and Cornwall Notes* and *Queries* [hereafter: DCNQ], 36, part 9 (spring, 1991), pp. 305-310 (quotation, p. 307).

[10] C. L'Estrange Ewen, *Witch-Hunting and Witch Trials* (New York, 1929), pp. 63-64.

[11] M. Stoyle, 'It is but an Old Witch Gone: Prosecution and Execution for Witchcraft in Exeter, 1558-1610', *History*, volume 96, no. 322 (April 2011), pp. 137-38.

[12] Ibid., pp. 138-39.

[13] Ibid., p. 139.

[14] Ibid., pp. 139-40.

[15] B. Rosen, *Witchcraft in England, 1558-1618* (Amherst, Massachusetts, 1991), pp. 54-56; and J. Sharpe, *Witchcraft in Early Modern England* (2001), p. 16.

[16] Stoyle, 'It is but an Old Witch Gone', pp. 140-41.

[17] Ibid., pp. 141-42.

[18] Rosen, *Witchcraft in England*, p. 67.

[19] Ibid., pp. 67-69.

[20] M. Stoyle, 'The Execution of a Witch in Elizabethan Exeter', *DCNQ*, volume 40, Part 7 (spring, 2010), pp. 195-99; and Stoyle, 'It is but an Old Witch Gone', pp. 142-44.

[21] Ibid.

[22] M. Stoyle, 'Two New Seventeenth-Century Witch Cases from Exeter', *DCNQ*, volume 40, part 6 (autumn 2009), pp. 163-66; and Stoyle, 'It is but an Old Witch Gone', pp. 143-46.

[23] Sharpe, *Instruments*, p. 48.

[24] Rosen, *Witchcraft*, pp. 57-58.

[25] Stoyle, 'Two New Seventeenth-Century Witch Cases', pp. 163, 166-73; and Stoyle, 'It is but an Old Witch Gone', pp. 143-46.

[26] Ibid.

[27] J. S. Cockburn, *A History of English Assizes, 1558-1714* (Cambridge, 1972), pp. 120, 228.

[28] M. Stoyle, 'Witchcraft in Exeter: The Cases of John and Elizabeth Crosse', *DCNQ*, volume 41, part 7 (spring, 2015), p. 197.

[29] Ibid., pp. 197-98; and - for transcriptions and translations of the original indictments - pp. 200-203.

[30] M. Stoyle, 'Witchcraft in Exeter: The Case of Widow Stone, 1619-20', *DCNQ*, Volume 40, Part 9 (spring, 2011), pp. 259-60.

[31] The most well-known English witch to have suffered this terrible fate was Margery Jurdemayne, burnt in 1441, but it is significant to note that she was burnt as both a witch and 'a heretic', see P.G. Maxwell-Stuart, *The British Witch: The Biography* (Stroud, 2014), p. 73.

32 For the process by which the trial of accused witches came to be 'overwhelmingly the province of the assize courts' after 1590 or thereabouts, see G. Durston, *Witchcraft and Witch-Trials: A History of English Witchcraft and its Legal Perspectives, 1542-1736* (Chichester, 2000), pp. 191-93 (quotation, p. 193).

33 For transcriptions of these depositions, see Stoyle, 'Case of the Widow Stone', pp. 260-62.

34 Ibid., p. 260.

35 Ibid.

36 Ibid., p. 259.

37 ECA, Book 61, f. 218.

38 D. Underdown, 'The Taming of the Scold: The Enforcement of Patriarchal Authority in Early Modern England', in A. Fletcher and J. Stevenson (eds), *Order and Disorder in Early Modern England* (Cambridge, 1985), pp. 119-120, and 123-25.

39 ECA, Book 62, f.2v.

40 See table in Sharpe, *Instruments*, p. 109.

41 Stoyle, 'Cases of John and Elizabeth Crosse', p. 204.

42 On 'cunning folk', see K. Thomas, *Religion and the Decline of Magic: Studies in Popular Belief in Sixteenth and Seventeenth Century England* (1971, London, 1997 edition), pp. 212-52.

43 Stoyle, 'Cases of John and Elizabeth Crosse', p. 204.

44 For the site of the Little Conduit, see M. Stoyle, *Water in the City: The Aqueducts and Underground Passages of Exeter* (Exeter, 2014), pp. 105-108

45 Stoyle, 'Cases of John and Elizabeth Crosse', p. 204.

46 Ibid.

47 Ibid., pp. 203-04.

48 Ibid., pp. 199-200.

49 Ibid.

50 ECA, Exeter Quarter Sessions Rolls [hereafter: EQSR], 4-5 Charles I, roll dated 21 April 1628, indictment relating to Sith Coleman.

51 Ibid.

52 DHC, 3429A/PR/1/1 (Parish Register of St Sidwell's, Exeter, unpaginated), entry of 14 April 1656.

53   ECA, Book 62, f.316v.

54   Ibid., f.340. For Pentecost Edie's date of birth, see DHC, F. Nesbitt (transcriber), 'Exeter Parish Registers: St Edmunds' (three handwritten volumes, 1932), I, p. 19.

55   The word 'jade' was used by contemporaries to refer to an unchaste or shameless woman; for some further local instances of this usage, see T. Gray, *Strumpets and Ninnycocks: Name Calling in Devon, 1540-1640* (Exeter, 2016), pp. 188-89.

56   ECA, Book 62, ff.340-340v.

57   Nesbitt, 'St Edmund's Registers', II, p. 13; and Nesbitt, 'St Edmund's Registers', III, p. 41.

58   For subsequent references to Caselie and the Edies, see Nesbitt, 'St Edmund's Registers', II, p. 15; Nesbitt, 'St Edmund Registers', I, pp. 40, 43; and Nesbitt, 'St Edmund's Registers', III, pp. 42 and 48.

59   See ECA, Books 62 and 63, passim.

60   Sharpe, *Instruments*, pp. 126-27.

61   Ibid., pp. 109, 127. See also Sharpe, *Witchcraft in Early Modern England*, p. 30; and Ewen, *Witch-Trials*, p. 107.

62   See M. Stoyle, *From Deliverance to Destruction: Rebellion and Civil War in an English City* (Exeter, 1996), pp. 47-61.

63   Ibid., pp. 69-74.

64   ECA, Book 64, f.27v.

65   Ibid; and ECA, EQSR, 1641-42, roll 4.

66   See M.J. Stoyle, 'Whole Streets Converted to Ashes: Property Destruction in Exeter during the English Civil War', *Southern History*, 16 (1994), pp. 67-84.

67   ECA, Book 64, f.96v.

68   Intriguingly, on this occasion Lendon was said to have predicted that great fires would soon take place within the city. See ECA, Book 64, f.179.

69   See M. Gaskill, *Witchfinders: A Seventeenth Century English Tragedy* (2005), passim; and, for a recent estimate of the total number killed, M. Braddick, *God's Fury: England's Fire: A New History of the English Civil Wars* (2008), p. 428.

70   For executions of witches elsewhere in England during the late 1640s and 1650s, see Ewen, *Witch Hunting*, p. 108; *Sharpe, Instruments*, table, p. 109;

and Sharpe, *Witchcraft in Early Modern England*, pp. 72-73. For previous treatments of some of the Exeter witch-cases of the 1650s, see W. Cotton and H. Woolcombe, *Gleanings from the Municipal and Cathedral Records Relating to Exeter* (Exeter, 1877), pp. 149-52; and J. Thompson, *Wives, Widows, Witches and Bitches: Women in Seventeenth-Century Devon* (New York, 1993), pp. 101-27, and 191-95.

[71] ECA, Book 64, f.200v.

[72] Ibid.

[73] Ibid., f.201.

[74] Ibid.

[75] Rosen, *Witchcraft*, pp. 70-71; and ECA, Book 61, ff.52 and 378.

[76] ECA, Book 64, ff.182v and 286.

[77] ECA, Book 64, f.201.

[78] Ibid., f.226.

[79] Ibid., f.243. For the original indictment against Crosse, see ECA, EQSR, 1651-55, bundle endorsed 'Easter Sessions and Gaol Delivery 1654'.

[80] ECA, Book 64, f.243.

[81] Ibid., ff. 260v-261v.

[82] Ibid., f.261v.

[83] Ibid., f.260v.

[84] Ibid. ff.260v-261.

[85] Ibid., f.261v.

[86] Ewen, *Witch-Hunting*, pp. 62-63.

[87] ECA, Book 64, f.261.

[88] Ibid., f.260.

[89] Ibid., f.274.

[90] See ECA, EQSR, 1655-57, bundle labelled '1656', for the indictment against Babbage.

[91] ECA, Book 64, f.411-411v. Cole duly appeared at the next sessions, and was 'discharged', see ECA, EQSR, 1657-1660, bundle endorsed 'Michaelmas Sessions ... 1658', recognisance relating to Ambrose Cole.

[92] ECA, Book 64, ff.419v-420.

[93] Ibid.

[94] Ibid.

[95] See ECA, EQSR, 1657-1660, bundle endorsed 'Xmas Sessions ... January 1658[9]', recognisance and indictment relating to Joan Taylor.

[96] ECA, Book 64, f.430v.

[97] Ibid.

[98] Ibid. For a definition of the dialect word 'creemed', see Devoniensis, 'An Exmoor Vocabulary', *The Gentleman's Magazine*, volume 16 (August, 1746). 'Creemed by the fairies' is perhaps the Devonian equivalent of the Scottish term 'elf-grippit', for which see E. Wilby, *Cunning Folk and Familiar Spirits: Shamanistic Visionary Traditions in Early Modern British Witchcraft and Magic* (Eastbourne, 2010), p. 21.

[99] For laying-on of hands, see Wilby, *Cunning Folk*, p. 34.

[100] ECA, Book 64, f.430v; and ECA, EQSR, bundle endorsed 'Xmas Sessions ... January 1658[9]', recognisance and indictment relating to Joan Furnace.

[101] Sharpe, *Witchcraft in Early Modern England*, p. 74.

[102] ECA, Book 65, ff. 1v-4.

[103] For another witch-case brought before the city magistrates in November 1660, this time involving two suspected witches from South Tawton in Devon who had recently been released from the High Gaol, see ECA, Book 65, ff. 11-11v and 15v-16.

[104] *Calendar of State Papers, 1682*, p. 347 (quotation); and R. North, *The Life of the Right Honourable Francis North, Baron of Guildford* (1742), pp. 129-30.

[105] Barry, *Witchcraft and Demonology*, p. 68.

[106] Anon., 'Exeter Police', *Western Times* (16 September 1837).

[107] For a study of the persistence of witch-belief in Somerset, which reveals many fascinating parallels with witch-belief in early modern Exeter, see O. Davies, *A People Bewitched: Witchcraft and Magic in Nineteenth-Century Somerset* (Trowbridge, 1999).

[108] ECA, Book 100, f.22.

[109] ECA, Act Book IV, f. 137.

[110] ECA, Miscellaneous Roll 20, m.2.

[111] Ibid., m.3.

[112] Ibid.

[113] ECA, EQSR, 23 Elizabeth I; indictments transcribed and translated in M. Stoyle. 'The Execution of a Witch in Elizabethan Exeter', *DCNQ*, volume 40, part 7 (spring, 2010), pp. 196-98.

[114] Miscellaneous Roll, 20, m.22v.

[115] ECA, EQSR, 44 Elizabeth I; indictments transcribed and translated in M. Stoyle, 'Two New Seventeenth Century Witch Cases from Exeter', DCNQ, volume 40, part VI (Autumn, 2009), pp. 163-66.

[116] ECA, EQSR, 8 James I; indictments transcribed and translated in Stoyle, 'Two New Seventeenth Century Witch Cases', pp. 166-73.

[117] ECA, EQSR, 13 James 1; indictments transcribed and translated in M. Stoyle, 'Witchcraft in Exeter: The Cases of John and Elizabeth Crosse', *DCNQ*, volume 41, Part VII (Spring, 2015), pp. 200-203.

[118] ECA, Book 61, f.218.

[119] Ibid., ff. 459-466; depositions transcribed in M. Stoyle, 'Witchcraft in Exeter: The case of the Widow Stone, 1619-20', *DCNQ*, volume 40, part 9 (Spring, 2011), pp. 259-62.

[120] ECA, EQSR, 2-3 Charles I.

[121] ECA, EQSR, 4-5 Charles I.

[122] ECA, Book 64, f. 27v.

[123] Ibid, f. 96v.

[124] Ibid., ff. 200-201, 226-227.

[125] Ibid., f.242; and ECA, EQSR, Box for 1654-55, bundle labelled '1653-54'.

[126] ECA, EQSR, Box for 1654-55, bundle labelled '1654'.

[127] ECA, EQSR, Box for 1655-57, bundle labelled '1656'.

[128] Book 64, f. 411v.

[129] Ibid, f. 420.

[130] ECA, EQSR, Box for 1657-60, bundle labelled 'Xmas sessions held the x of January 1658(9)'.

[131] Book 64, f.430.

[132] EQSR, Box for 1657-60, bundle labelled 'Xmas sessions held the x of January 1658(9)'.

[133] ECA, Book 65, ff. 1v-4.

[134] Ibid., ff. 11-11v, 15v-16.

Index